ONE STEP TO A PORN FREE LIFE

QUIANDRA E. JAMES

DR. NES INTERNATIONAL CONSULTING & PUBLISHING

LOS ANGELES COUNTY, CA

Copyright © 2019 One Step To a Porn Free Life by Quiandra E. James.
All rights reserved.

Dr. Nes International Consulting & Publishing
P.O. Box 70167
Pasadena, CA 91117
www.drnesintl.com

All rights reserved. No part of this publication may be reproduced, stored in a retrieval system, or transmitted in any form or by any means—for example, electronic, photocopy, recording—without the prior written permission of the author and/or publisher. The only exception is brief quotations in printed reviews.

Unless otherwise indicated, all scripture quotations are taken from The King James Version/Amplified Bible Parallel Edition Copyright 1995 by The Zondervan Corporation and the Lockman Foundation. All rights reserved.

ISBN: 978-1-949461-10-7

Senior Editor: Kia Stokes, M.B.A
Cover Design: Jessica Land

DEDICATION

This book is dedicated to my husband Reginald James, who made it his duty to push me forward in getting this book done. Without him and his prayers this book would have never been a finished product. I also want to dedicate this book to every family member and friend that encouraged me when I wanted to give up. I am so grateful for my tribe.

All blank pages are intentional

One Step to a Porn Free Life
TABLE OF CONTENTS

CHAPTER 1: CLOSING DOORS 7

CHAPTER 2: IDENTIFYING ROOTS 19

CHAPTER 3: BORDERS 31

CHAPTER 4: IT'S A LIE! 49

CHAPTER 5: BAGGAGE CLAIM 61

CHAPTER 6: WHAT'S THAT SMELL? 75

CHAPTER 7: CONCLUSION 91

MEET THE AUTHOR 97

CONTACT 99

QUIANDRA JAMES

All blank pages are intentional

One Step to a Porn Free Life

1
CLOSING DOORS

I want to bring you into my life throughout this book because it is important that you see the progression of where my pornography addiction was taking me. Leading up to the moment where I became free from my pornography addiction, I spent a lot of time fixated on the next time and moment I was going to be able to watch porn, and without being interrupted by anyone. Pornography became my best friend. It was the one thing that distracted me from my thoughts and the one thing that demanded most of my attention. I began to need it and it was the one thing that made me feel like no one has ever made me feel, which was wanted...until I got to college. When I got to college, I became a part of this gospel group on my campus called Psalms 150. There I began to learn about God in a way where I no longer could pretend, I knew Him or that I loved Him. It was in college that God started showing me that I proclaimed to love Him, but I was living a double life. I started to do risky things that could have caused me to go to jail, if I would have gotten caught. I also started drinking. I was spiraling down a path that was not God's will for me, and it was not who He created me to be. I saw that I no longer cared about whether I lived or died. To tell you the truth, in my soul, I felt like I was dying. I realized that a lot of my actions was connected to my porn addiction. I just kept having this feeling of guilt, but it really was God telling me that all those things I was doing was not me because it was not Him. God was patient with me until this one day where I had enough. The day I became tired of how my "best friend" porn left me, feeling empty, feeling confused, feeling hopeless, feeling filthy, and feeling stuck.

Then one day in March 2013, I was balling my eyes out. Just having one of my dramatic crying out to God moments because I once again fell into the trap of watching pornography and masturbating. This time was different from the rest because I understood that God had a greater plan for me. I understood that God wanted to help me, but only if I was willing to let Him. I didn't realize that when I was kid and was prayed over by my Grandmother when my family discovered my addiction to porn, I had no clue what to do next. There was no guidance and I still didn't know that God had already provided a way of escape from any type of lifestyle. At the age of 19, I knew what I was doing and that it was wrong. I knew that there was a solution to my problem, but I couldn't figure out what it would take to make that solution real for me. So, at 19 years old I surrendered to God. I no longer saw this as my problem that I had to fix myself, but I saw it as my problem that Christ was going to help me fix. I became vulnerable and allowed myself to be brought down to my knees. I was broken and realized that a broken vase cannot put itself back together, only the potter that created it, which is God.

By this time, I thought to myself, I bet God is tired of this routine of me falling back into porn after crying out to Him and me saying that I was done. I thought there had to be a point where God would give up and eventually give me over to my sin. Before I go any further, I want you to stop and get a Bible. You could search a Bible online if you don't have one. Trust me, it's going to be crucial on this journey we are taking together. I would like you to go to Romans 1:18-32. This is what I meant by God giving me over to my sin. The truth was that I knew better and I knew watching pornography as well as masturbating was wrong. How did I know that? I was worshipping myself. I was putting what I wanted above God. I had become my own idol as well as pornography. Since I knew that what I was doing was wrong, I knew that Romans 1:18-32 was leading down this path. I knew that continuing to sin despite knowing that it was not right was making me numb, therefore causing me to become nonchalant about other wrong things. For example, I started to look at women in a provocative way. I am a woman so I shouldn't look at woman in a sexual manner but me continuing to indulge in pornography had me to view women in a lustful way. Take a moment and just evaluate yourself. Look over your life. Maybe there are other things that may have not necessarily led you to porn, but other ungodly acts.

Are there any sins that you have committed that caused you to commit others? Maybe you struggle with porn? If so, what ways has your pornography addiction caused you to do other things that aren't right? Can you identify with any of the things in Romans 1:29 that you knew your pornography addiction played a part in?

Despite all of those thoughts I began to have about God being tired of me coming to Him, I humbled myself and went to God again anyway. I felt like what I was doing was not the real me. I didn't think God would hear me since I binged watched porn and masturbated the night before, but I still prayed. I said "Lord I'm really done with porn this time. Can you please take this taste out of my mouth? Please take this desire from me Jesus! I'm really done with pornography this time." God answered me back with a very profound question. God asked, "Are you really done this time?" I then replied, "Lord I am so serious. I'm ready to be done, whatever I have to do I'll do it." God then said, "Okay, I will do my part, but you have to promise me that you will do your part." So of course, I'm crying still and saying Lord whatever I have to do I'll do it, whatever it takes. God stood true to His Word and I have not desired to watch porn since that day. That was four years ago.

Despite that one decision changing the course of my life, there were a lot of struggles that I had in those four years. There were some hard decisions I had to make too. I didn't know the strings that were attached to watching pornography until after I got free from the addiction. Can I just be real with you guys? One of the struggles was I still desired to masturbate and I did. I would masturbate and still feel dirty, like I did after I watched pornography. Can you relate to that? Another struggle was I would read sexual books like the *50 Shades* and *Zane* books, that allowed me to imagine the sexual experiences I wanted. Eventually, I started to feel dirty from that too. Then I was experimenting with a sex toy. Do you see a pattern? I was trading in one thing for another, but this time God gave me grace. He didn't allow me to become addicted to my struggles in the four years, like I was addicted to pornography. Instead, once I surrendered to Him, He started quickly convicting me about the things I was doing. It was in such a loving way too. It was as if Jesus was saying, "No, daughter. I don't desire for you to do that either, because those things will lead you away from My purpose for your life. Serve Me, not you. Focus on Me, and not on what your flesh likes." There was a constant back and forth between me and God. I really got to build a relationship with Him through this process. Once I no longer saw Him as my slave master who wanted to whip me whenever I did wrong, I started to see Him as my Father who wanted nothing but His best for me. Take a moment to examine yourself. Do you believe that God's best for you is for you to be addicted to pornography or anything else all your life? Do you think that God wants to help you and not punish you like a slave master? Do you believe that God loves you despite your mistakes? Do you believe you can get out of this addiction or any addiction with Christ?

God can do something so profound for you just like He did for me. He did it. But I can't deny the fact that I also had to put some work into making sure I remained free. Do you ever find yourself having these feelings of disgust, dirtiness, dissatisfaction, or emptiness after watching porn or committing sin? Do you ever find yourself at a point where you want to stop but then you have those thoughts of, "Are you really done with this? Are you sure you can leave this alone?" If your answer is yes, then I'm glad you are still reading. I believe God wants you to be free, but I can't lie and say that you can be free without Him. Obtaining true freedom is tougher without Him.

What I desire more than anything is for anyone who reads this book to know that they are not alone in this struggle of being addicted to pornography. Not only that, but I recognize how hard it is to break free from it once you have done it for an extended amount of years. Know that there is no condemnation in Christ Jesus (Read Romans 8:1) and if you feel God tugging at your heart after reading this book, that is Him convicting you. Conviction means that you feel in your heart that what you are doing is not really who you are or who God called you to be. Any shame or guilt is from the enemy. The enemy wants you to feel you aren't able to go to God with this addiction and receive the grace that Christ died on the cross for you to have. I am here to tell you that the gift of grace and mercy is yours, FOR FREE, waiting for you to take it. God knew you would need it this day and that you would need that grace the rest of your life. Every single day I wake up and thank God for His grace and His mercy on me because I recognize that I need a Savior to save me daily. I will never "arrive" but every day I take the time to go to God to receive His grace so that I can remain free from porn as well as all sin. I am in this with you. I said all of that to say that I want you to do the same. Choose this day to receive Christ's death as covering for your sin, to choose life over death, to choose grace over guilt, and to choose to accept God's gift and reject your flesh. I know this may be the hardest choice of your life, but YOU ARE WORTH IT. You deserve to live a life full of God's blessings and to be all that He has called you to be. To be honest, it is impossible to walk that out when you have one foot in the world and one foot in God's path for your life. It's even harder when you don't even know Him or believe in Jesus as your Lord and Savior. I know at this point you're probably thinking, "I thought this book is supposed to be about pornography", but this addiction goes way deeper. The questions I want you to answer when you finish reading this book is, who will I choose? Will I continue to choose to serve myself or will I choose to serve God? It's time to choose.

Since I have you thinking, I want you to get somewhere comfortable away from distractions. I want you to ask yourself, "Do I like the person I have become? If not, why not?" This is an opportunity for you to give it all to Christ. This is the time for you to open your mouth and ask God to help you. Give it all to Him right now. He is the only one that can take your burdens in exchange for peace. Try it. What's the worst that can happen?

One Step to a Porn Free Life

Reflections
Questions

1. What has been your greatest challenge in combatting pornography?

2. Closing doors is about committing to stopping what you used to do so you can move forward in freedom. What is a commitment(s) that you can make to yourself during this process?

3. What are some doors that you think you need to close in order to move forward in becoming free from pornography addiction?

Reflections

One Step to a Porn Free Life

Reflections

2
IDENTIFYING THE ROOT

On this journey of becoming free from pornography, I recognized that pornography was just a surface problem that I had. God revealed to me that there was a deeper issue that I needed to bring to light and uproot. One of those deeply rooted issues was the lust and perversion in my family. Let me share a little background story. While one of my family babysat me, it was they turned on porn. It was then the seed was planted in me. However, before I watched my first porno, I had this dream that I was in bed with one of my male family members that was supposed to be watching me. From what I can recall, we didn't do anything but we both were just in the bed. I could never figure out what that dream meant and honestly, as a kid I thought it was real and assumed that that family member violated me in some way. Up until I was 23 years old, God revealed what He was showing me. He was warning me that I was going to be involved in something with this family member that would be a struggle. I was so blown away by this. It was amazing to me that God spoke to me through dreams at four years old, even though I didn't take heed to the warning at that time. This dream also helped me to see that what I was dealing with was a generational struggle of lust and perversion.

I want to take a moment to encourage those out there who don't believe God speaks to you or can speak to you. He can and He does. Young or old, God speaks to all of us, and in different ways. Some of you may have dreams, visions, some have a level of "knowing" or discernment," which is the Holy Spirit letting you in on knowing things about people that they did not tell you. Some of you sense things like, if your friend has anxiety you start to feel anxious when you're around them or you can taste things that you did not eat. There are so many ways that God speaks. God may speak to you through other people or speak to you through reading the Bible. I want you to take a moment and think about this. Get in a space where there are no distractions so you can really evaluate this question. I promise this will get you excited for God to speak to you more. What are ways that God may be communicating to you and you don't even realize it?

After realizing what the dream meant, I came to a conclusion. Not to blame any of my family for passing this generational curse down, but I had to acknowledge that lust and perversion was a real problem for me. Once I recognized how it was a real struggle in my family, on both sides, I was determined to stop it. I first started analyzing things that I've been through that could have opened the door for the devil to tempt me with lust in the first place. I asked myself questions such as "What was going on in my childhood around 4-5?" "What led me to continue with watching porn and eventually masturbating?" "Was it rejection from my parents or my family?" "Was it that I felt I had to be perfect?"

What I found out was I was a rejected child who searched for the need to "feel good" and "feel wanted." I felt abandoned as a child by my father, my mother, and even my family. Even though I had all of them around me, they might as well not have been there. I felt abandoned by my dad because he kept choosing other women over my mom, my siblings, and me. As a young child, I didn't know why my dad couldn't just choose us over them. I felt abandoned by my mother because she kept choosing to be with my father despite his infidelity and abuse. I had a lot of thoughts of why she wasn't choosing my siblings and me over him. I felt abandoned by my family because I knew they knew what was going on in our household but were barely helping. As a grownup I know some of this wasn't true, but it doesn't take away from the fact that I felt that way back then. I also discovered that I felt pornography was the only thing I had control over in my life, which was a flat out lie from the enemy. I thought I could stop and start when I wanted, because I had control over nothing else in my life. Sadly, I soon found out that I couldn't. Pornography had control over me. I honestly saw myself as no different as a crack addict or an alcoholic; in which when I think about it, is the same just a different addiction.

When looking at the root cause of my pornography addiction, I realized that rejection was a huge part of my of it. The definition of rejection is to repel, throwback, or refuse to hear. Rejection was the seed planted because my parents had been through a lot together and I felt like I could never be a child. Instead, I had to play the role as an adult, especially to my siblings. I felt like I was there for my parents more than they were there for me. I felt like the love I was wanting; my parents weren't available to give it to me because they were too caught up in each other's drama. It wasn't until I got older and God started taking me through a process of healing and forgiving my parents, that I found out I had a lot of mother wounds as well as father wounds.

One Step to a Porn Free Life

Mother wounds meaning, there were things that my mother did, said, didn't do, or didn't say that really hurt me. Father wounds was the same. The crucial part was that it became a wound because I did not deal with how the rejection made me feel. I preferred to numb the pain and pornography did that for me. It gave me a distraction from what I really was struggling with on the inside. My dad was the type that if I didn't do anything perfect then he would verbally abuse me. If I ate too much in his eyes, he would put me down, or if I was just clumsy, he would yell at me. I felt like I could never get it right no matter how hard I tried. I also didn't like how he would treat my mother. I was the type of child where if you would do it to my mother, you might as well have done it to me. I just didn't understand how he could say he loved my mother but would fight with her or cheat on her regularly. I felt as if we were not good enough to do right by.

As I have gotten older, I have a greater understanding that my daddy's struggles were way deeper than that. I also struggled with rejection from my mother because I didn't understand why she kept going back to my father after he kept hurting us. I felt like my mother constantly chose him over us, and again as I got older, I found out that when you're married that's what you're supposed to do. Once my mother finally left my dad, I started to feel rejected by her working and going to school. The cycle of rejection just continued. I felt like I had no one, not my mother or my father. But pornography was always there anytime I needed or wanted it; it never rejected me. When I was lonely it was there, when I needed to relieve stress it was there, when I was bored it was there, and when I just wanted it was there; it never made me feel less than or like I had to be this perfect person. It was my safe space. I could be whoever I wanted to be when watching pornography. I never had to beg for it. The lust and perversion from pornography quenched my thirst every time until...it didn't the next minute. Have you ever had a taste for something sweet and then you get something sweet but then you want more sweets? How about wanting to watch a television show on Netflix and after you watch one episode you just can't stop until you have binged watched the whole series? That's how pornography made me feel. Even though it satisfied me one minute, the next I wanted more because I never wanted the feeling pornography gave me to end. Pornography never rejected me.

There was so many more emotional struggles that I saw played a part in pornography being able to draw me in. Honestly, I believe that if those seeds of rejection would not have been planted in my childhood, that open door to pornography would have not remained opened. "IF THE SEED WASN'T PLANTED THE DOOR WOULDN'T HAVE MATTERED." Imagine if you loved on your child and made sure to always plant seeds of love and positivity into your child. Wouldn't you think that if a boy/girl came and tried to give your child false love, your child wouldn't open that door? That's what I think about rejection.

There were so many seeds of rejection planted into my life that I welcomed pornography with opened arms once that door was open.

As you are going through your journey of breaking free, I want you to consider some of your own hang-ups. Get somewhere really comfortable and without distractions. Consider some of these questions:

- What was your relationship like with your parents when you started to watch pornography?
- What was going on around you when you started to watch pornography or before/after?
- Was there any physical abuse, sexual abuse, emotional abuse, or verbal abuse that you experienced?
- How did you get introduced to pornography?
- Was pornography a way for you to get away from what was going on in your life or cope with life?

If your answer is yes to any of these questions, there is a high likelihood that you are dealing with generational struggles that you may have not known about. You may struggle with rejection/bitterness from your past that you have not dealt with but maybe it was passed down from your mother or your father. Generational struggles are sins, that you notice, that have been passed down from generation to generation in your family. Sins you saw/heard your daddy, your grandfather, your great-grandmother, etc. struggled with. Not only that, but you also see it playing out in your own life. For example, I just found out this year that my maternal great-grandfather committed suicide. That was a generational curse of death that was passed down to me. When things got hard dealing with this addiction, my thought was to commit suicide.

By the time God revealed all of the things above to me, I immediately thought, "I'm a train wreck." Maybe you're having the same thoughts right now. I want you to know it's okay. God showed me that no matter what I have been through God loves me. The same goes for you. This world is full of people who make crazy decisions and we get caught up in them, but God is faithful. HE WILL NEVER LEAVE YOU. He is not like the world. He wants you to experience freedom and He wants to walk with you through this process. He is your Great Shepherd ready to lead you His sheep into the right direction. Will you follow Him? Please read Psalm 23.

One Step to a Porn Free Life

Reflections
Questions

1. What do you believe is the key event that lead you to begin watching pornography?

2. Did you ever address what happened to you or around you, in regard to that key event? If so, what were the results? If not, be honest, what has kept you from addressing what happened?

3. I know it's tough thinking about all of the wrong you've done and even the wrong that has been done to you; just remember that isn't who you are. Reflect on the scripture Romans 8. Write out who God says you are, in that scripture.

Reflections

One Step to a Porn Free Life

Reflections

QUIANDRA JAMES

3
BORDERS

Let's discuss boundaries. Before I get into this subject, I once heard a story about fire. The story was that fire in a fireplace, a contained space, is a safe area to have a fire. On the other hand, a fire that starts in the forest is a dangerous fire because it has nothing to contain it to keep it from spreading. For example, the forest fires that have been happening in California. The United States of America has what seems to be an unlimited supply of water, yet those fires were spreading despite the firefighters attempting to put them out. Because those fires were not contained, they were extremely hard to put out.

Sexual desire is just like fire. If you contain it in marriage then it's safe but when you give into your sexual desires outside of your husband/wife, it becomes out of control. The way we contain our sexual desires is by having boundaries. 2 Timothy 2:22 says, "Run away from youthful lusts—pursue righteousness, faith, love, and peace with those [believers] who call on the Lord out of a pure heart." To break this down, you desiring to watch pornography is youthful lust, but you establishing boundaries is you pursuing what's righteous, pursuing faith, pursuing love, and pursuing peace. The reason I want you to establish boundaries is because I want you to pursue and experience peace that you've never had before. I want you to pursue and experience love that you've never had before.

It is healthy to desire sex but, like I said before, it must only be in the context of a man and a woman in marriage. Everybody's boundaries are different because what may cause one person to desire sex may not cause another person to desire sex. Some boundaries include: accountability, getting a mentor/therapist, throwing things away that remind you of your past, being mindful of the company you keep, being careful of who you follow on social media, joining Celebrate Recovery, joining Pornography Anonymous meetings, being careful about the music you listen to, being careful about the type of content you are reading, and paying attention to where you spend most of your time. This is the time where you have to sit down and evaluate your triggers.

A trigger is something you see, hear, taste, touch, or smell that causes you to desire sex; which in our case causes you to then desire to watch pornography. I'll give you some examples of my triggers. Can we just take a second to talk about R&B? Some of my favorite singers are Tank, Jamie Foxx, Chris Brown (before 2012), and so many more. I loved R&B and Soul. I loved Hip Hop too. Some of my favorite artists were Lil Wayne, Tupac, Common, Ludacris, etc. I was just a music fanatic growing up. No one could pay me to stop listening to R&B/Soul, Hip Hop, Pop, and some Gospel back in the day. Until one day I gave God my yes to doing whatever it took to make sure I remained free from my pornography addiction.

It was like after that moment, I became so sensitive to the music I was listening to that I actually started paying attention to the lyrics that a lot of those artists were singing. Let's just say I was so disappointed, but I was so determined to remain free that I just made that choice to not listen to secular music for a while. So, I went on about a 6- month journey of only listening to gospel music and was even introduced to Christian rap. I didn't know how much secular music makes you want to do some sinful things or think about doing them, until I stopped listening to it. Some questions to ask yourself: What things are being produced in your life today due to the music you listen to? Are they good things or bad things? Do the things you listen to give you a desire to watch pornography? Does the music lead you to want to live a pornography free life? Does the music you listen to give you hope and freedom? Does the music you listen to aid in you numbing the pain/disappointment you feel towards your addiction? Does the music you listen to enable you to do what you know is wrong or does it give you a desire to live a life pleasing to God?

I also took a break from social media because as you know, we live in an overly sexual world to where now you can swipe up on IG and there will be a half-naked woman on the explore page. I knew I was in a crucial time in my life where I couldn't have anything making me stumble back into my old patterns, so I cut it. My freedom was priceless, plus most of the people I followed at that time wasn't talking about anything anyway. I cut out watching certain television shows that promoted being overly sexual like Love and Hip Hop, The Kardashians, The Real Housewives, Bad Girls Club, and a number of others. Again, my freedom was priceless to me, plus all those people cared about was that check. They are not worried about how their dressing half-naked or wearing super tight jeans that show the imprint of your private area (for men) may possibly make Quiandra relapse back into her pornography addiction. So, I had to choose me just like they were. Some questions I want you to ask yourself: What things are being produced in your life due to the social media you look at and the people you follow? Are they good things or bad things? Do who you follow on social media keep you stuck in your pornography addiction or cause you to desire to watch it? Do who you follow on social media give you a desire to live a life free from pornography addiction? Does social media enable you in finding a distraction, running away from dealing with your pornography addiction?

I am not ashamed to admit that I was an avid reader of sexual books. I owned the Zane books, I had all *50 Shades of Grey* books, and other sexual books by authors I can't remember the names of. I spent a lot of money on books when I would take a break from watching pornography. So, when the time came to get free from my pornography addiction, I threw all of those books away. For those of you who may be thinking why didn't you just sell them? I didn't sell them because I would be doing the same thing these authors were doing when they sold these books. I would be making people think about dirty things just like those books had me thinking dirty things. I refused to help someone else engage in reading a book that was basically pornography, so I put the books where they belonged and that was in the trash. Some questions to ask yourself: What things are being produced in your life today due to the things you read? Are they good things or bad things? Are they wise or are they foolish? Do the things you read give you a desire to watch pornography? Do the things you read give you a desire to masturbate or have sex? Do the things you read help you to grow and be a better you? Do the things you read give you a desire to be like Jesus Christ?

I don't know about you guys but back in the day, I had friends that just loved talking to me about their sex lives and sharing sex stories. When I recognized how unhealthy it was for me to be so intrigued by these stories, I began avoiding those friends (at that time in my life I didn't like conflict so instead of just saying don't tell me sex stories anymore I just avoided people.) I don't recommend avoiding people AT ALL because if we have someone that we call our friend we should be able to tell them that we don't want to hear their stories anymore, and they should be able to respect that. If they don't respect that then you have to draw the line and leave that friend alone; your freedom is worth it.

Some questions you can ask yourself:

- What things are being produced in your life today due to the friends you hang around?
- Are they good things or bad things?
- Do your friends promote your lifestyle, or do they encourage you to see how your actions keep you away from being who God wants you to be?

- Do you have any friends that will tell you that what you are doing is not who you really are?
- Do you have friends that never challenge you in growing and being a better person?
- Do you have friends that see the best in you and help to cultivate that? Do you have friends that are believers in Jesus Christ?

Now, I am not saying you have to do all the things that I did. God may lead you to do something different. I just knew that I was so deep into my pornography addiction that I had to make some drastic changes to stay out of it.

In addition to the above triggers, others were stress from work, stress from school, stress from my family, and even dating. Don't get scared, I'm not going to tell you that you can't take part in these things as long as you live. If you do choose to do that, that's between you and Jesus Christ. I'm just mentioning a few topics that will get you thinking about what some of your own triggers might be. Take a moment and get into a comfortable space without distraction. I want you to reflect back on things that cause you to desire to watch pornography. Is it loneliness? Is it boredom? Is it a person's body you see on social media? Is it that Usher song that reminds you of your first-time having sex? This is the time to get real with yourself and evaluate what really causes your mind to come to the conclusion that you want to watch pornography.

Now that you have made a list of your triggers, I want you to take the time to yourself or with someone you trust and see what type of boundaries you need to have. Since I was walking through this process alone, I invited the Holy Spirit in as my friend and allowed Him to tell me what type of boundaries or limitations should have around those triggers. For example, once I started getting back onto social media, I did a clean sweep of people that post vulgar things that I knew would be a stumbling block for me. It was a little tough because some of those people were people, I considered my friends, but I had to choose me over them. Another thing I did in regard to social media is I gave myself a social media bedtime. Do you know that there is nothing good going on at 1:00 a.m. on social media? Sometimes even when your page is full of Christians, at a certain time "Christians" get in their flesh and start posting or liking some sexual things. Instead of getting myself involved with that, I just shut it down.

Over time I was able to control my reaction to those types of posts. It took a good year and a half before I felt like I had gained some self-control to stay on social media past 10pm. Again, everyone is different, so you have to find out what works for you. This is why it is good to have God and your accountability partner to help you work through it.

One Step to a Porn Free Life

One more thing that I believe is very important is establishing boundaries while dating, building relationships, and being married. This may seem harsh, but I don't want to beat around the bush. If you are dating someone or just talking to someone and you guys are having sex outside of marriage, it is going to be hard to get free from a pornography addiction. The reason I say this is because pornography promotes sexual activity. So, if you're already engaged in sexual activity but trying to get free from pornography that can be a losing battle. Now in regard to a marriage, since you are able to have sex with your wife or husband, but you are addicted to pornography and desiring freedom, there needs to be a conversation with you, God, and your spouse.

I would even go further to say you may need to go to Christian counseling to get help in figuring out boundaries or seek out some wise counsel from people that you trust. They might be able to help you guys figure out steps in becoming free from your addiction. I can imagine that it's tough being married and your spouse of course desiring you sexually, but you are struggling with trying to break free from your pornography addiction which is tied to sex. Just know that all things are possible with God, as long as you have the faith to believe it is. God is able to restore and renew everything that was broken from you letting pornography into your marriage bed. You may be thinking why do I need to have my marriage bed restored and renewed? When you watch pornography, that's also creating soul ties with every single person you have watched. If you don't believe me, take the time to reflect on sex with your spouse. Do you ever have imaginations about pornography while you and your spouse are having sex? Do you feel the need to imagine or watch pornography before having sex with your spouse? Do you have a specific person that you like to watch? Do you remember the names of different pornography stars? These are signs that you have soul ties with those people. Think about it this way. If you are having sex with your spouse and you start imagining how sex was with your ex, would you consider that a soul tie? I just want you to recognize if there is anyone that you still have a sexual connection with outside of your spouse. If so, you have a soul tie with them because there is a bond there that should only be with your spouse.

The good news is that God is able to create a new fire and desire between you and your spouse, with your willingness to make things right. A fire that doesn't require you thinking about another person just to enjoy sex with your spouse, but a fire that causes you to want to learn your spouse sexually and become one with your spouse intimately. Just you, your spouse, and nobody else. If you just read that last line and you have the thought of "that's weird" or "that's boring", I suggest you email me for a great resource to get the spark back in your marriage. Again, this is for the MARRIED people. Not the "I got married in Mexico" or "I was in a relationship for 10 years, so I have a common law marriage."

I mean those who have a real marriage license that you and your spouse signed together.

Boundaries are so important for you. It requires a certain level of self-control and tenacity, but once you get to that point where you can let up just a little bit on your boundaries, you will praise God that you are not where you used to be. The only way to get there is by His grace. Jesus will grace you to get through this process, just trust Him.

Now let's discuss another very important topic that I wish I would have sought after, accountability. Let's first look at the definition for accountability.

Dictionary.com defines accountability as the state of being accountable, liable, or answerable. Having accountability is simply having someone to answer to. When seeking an accountability partner, don't just go to someone who you know won't really keep you accountable. If you are really seeking help on your freedom journey from your pornography addiction you need someone who you know will support you, and even pray for/with you. It may seem like this is tough because this step requires you to be vulnerable, open, and honest with someone or multiple people; depending on how much accountability you feel you need. In the long run, you're going to be grateful that you stepped out of your comfort zone and let someone into what your deep struggles are. Since you are going to be answering to this person, that means you will not only have to be honest with them about your struggles, but you will also have to share with them your triggers and boundaries list. This is needed because it's important for your accountability partner to know what they can keep you accountable to, so this exercise will help them to do that.

I know there are some people who may feel like they don't need people to keep them accountable and that's your personal preference. If that is how you feel, there are apps that can keep you accountable also. There is this app called Covenant Eyes that filters through your search engines on your cell phone and if you search something that seems like it may be related to pornography, they will have a virtual accountability partner contact you. There is also an app called Victory which is an app that helps you get a strategic plan together to help you fight against your pornography addiction. There is an online website called Fight The New Drug that has a bunch of resources, online support groups, and community events that you can join in regard to freedom from pornography addiction.

One Step to a Porn Free Life

Now stop and take a deep breath. I don't want you to feel that you have to do all of this in one day, unless you really feel you have to. This is an everyday journey of figuring out how to get free as well as how to remain free from your pornography journey. This is a journey of making mistakes and learning from them. This is a journey of crying because you want so badly to not do what your habit is. This is a journey of fighting for your freedom at any cost. Even though I don't desire to watch pornography anymore, God revealed to me that if I didn't take certain steps along the journey to stay free then I could possibly fall back into that addiction.

This is not to scare you but to humble you. Showing you that we are all in need of a Savior and we should take time daily to remain at the feet of Jesus Christ, laying down all of our sins that tries to make us fall back into old habits. Going to the feet of Jesus requires getting in a quiet space. Once you get into that quiet space, let Jesus know that you need to talk to Him. Going to the feet of Jesus is time spent where you get to just share with Him what's in your heart. You get to be as honest as you want with Him because unlike people, Jesus does not judge you. The truth is, Jesus already knows everything you're thinking so you might as well be honest with Him. He can only help you to the measure of how honest you are about the help you need. This is a time to speak to God but also to listen to see what He may tell you.

All believers in Jesus Christ need this every single day. Anytime you feel yourself getting to a point where you "got it together" and you don't need to go to God anymore, you don't need accountability, or you don't need to watch what you look at on social media, etc., check your heart. The word of God says in Proverbs 16:18 "Pride goes before destruction, and a haughty spirit before a fall." This means that when you begin to think that you can do life on your own, a fall and destruction is coming. Please stay humble my brothers and sisters. Keep your heart open to God in this journey and to the boundaries you have set.

One Step to a Porn Free Life

Reflections
Questions

1. Having freedom and not knowing what to do with that freedom comes with a cost. What have noticed in your life are costs to not doing the right things with your freedom and even indulging in the wrong things?

2. What are borders that you can begin to place in your life so that you can move forward in your journey of freedom?

3. List four of your strengths and three of your weaknesses. Be intentional about using the strengths during this journey of freedom. As for weaknesses, reflect on ways to make them strengths during this journey. Who do you know that your weaknesses are their strengths? Seek wisdom from them and look for scriptures that will give you wisdom.

Reflections

One Step to a Porn Free Life

Reflections

QUIANDRA JAMES

4
IT'S A LIE!

Can we take a quick moment to discuss the lies the devil may tell you? John 10:10 says, "A thief [the devil] is only there to steal and kill and destroy. I [Jesus Christ] came so they [you] can have real and eternal life, more and better life than they ever dreamed of." What I hope to help you understand is that you have an enemy and his name is satan. As the above scripture says, satan does not desire for you to have anything good in life, and all he wants is bad for you. So, I think it is very important that you know ways he will seek to destroy you in your journey of walking out completely in your freedom. I am talking about shame, guilt, and condemnation. These are 3 lies satan loves to use to keep you in your struggles. A lot of times it can happen without you even realizing it. I'm going to be honest and say these 3 things were the very things that kept me in my pornography addiction. I would mess up, then I would feel shameful because I knew it was wrong. When the guilt kicked it in, I would stop. It didn't last long though, and I would do it all over again. It was a cycle that had me spiraling to destruction. A cycle that had me spiritually dying, depressed, and suicidal.

For a long time, I had issues with committing to God and continuing a relationship with Him because whenever I messed up in any area, I felt this guilt that would cause me to run from God for at least two weeks. Guilt is feeling unworthy and not deserving of something. I felt unworthy of God's love because I wasn't perfect. I felt like I didn't deserve His love because I let Him down and myself down so many times. It was a horrible cycle that I was in up until I realized that I am a son of God and have been adopted by Him through the death of Jesus Christ.

When I say a son of God, I literally mean just like you are your mother's/father's child, we are all God's children. Realizing that I was God's child was crucial to my journey because again just like natural parents, no matter how many mistakes you make your parents will not throw you away. Their love for you is permanent and it is unconditional.

One Step to a Porn Free Life

I don't know about you, but I've done some things that my parents could have threw me away and said I was never going to be anything. But they never did. God never does either. God will never throw you away. Even if your parents did throw you away, the truth remains that God will NEVER throw you away. The scripture John 3:16, says that He gave His only Son for you so what else would he not do for you.

No matter what I do and what you do, God loves you. There may be consequences that come with those mistakes, but His love remains. He never changes up on you. Once I realized that, it completely freed me because not only did I count on me making mistakes since I am human, but I also found myself trying my best to live a life pleasing to God. I wanted to please Him from a place of love, not a place of fear of punishment or not being perfect. God is not a master waiting to punish us, but He is a loving Father who is waiting for us to run to Him, so He can receive us just like the Prodigal son's father received him. I can't lie and say that there won't be any consequences to our sin because there very well may be.

Whether we see them show up now or later, but even in the midst of that, we can trust that God will get us through it. Romans 6:23 says, "For the wages of sin is death, but the gift of God is eternal life in Christ Jesus our Lord." When we sin, it causes us to be spiritually dead inside. Numb to the world. Numb to pain. Sin can cause us to be angry and hate people. Sin can cause us to want to do things we never thought we would do. That is the death described in this scripture. When we accept that Jesus Christ died so that we may be free from everything that is not love, joy, peace, patience, kindness, goodness, faithfulness, long-suffering, and self-control...that's when we are free to say to God, "Yes I made a mistake but I don't want to live like this. I will not receive the shame from my sin, but I will receive grace. God show me what to do to get help with this. I am weak and I need you to make me strong."

Going even deeper, let's discuss guilt, shame, and condemnation from your past. Anyone who's reading this right now I want you to go get a pen and some paper, so you can do an activity. I want you to write down anything you've done in the past that you have held onto and haven't forgiven yourself for. This is something I really want you to spend some time on and write it all out on paper. This is between you and God so you can be as transparent as you want to be. I actually encourage you to be brutally honest. After you finish writing it all out, I want you to take some time to confess your sins to the Lord, or even to someone you trust if you want to.

At the end say, "I confess that these are sins I've committed in the past, but I want to turn away from them. I repent today Father and I ask that you forgive me Lord. I also speak that I forgive myself and I will no longer hold onto any guilt, shame, or condemnation that the devil may try to put on me. My slate has been wiped clean and I receive God's grace and His mercy today. In Jesus Christ name I pray AMEN!" Once that's done you can do whatever you want with the papers; keep them, burn them, etc. Whatever you feel will be a physical representation of the spiritual release you have just spoken. Now satan will try to bring these things back to your remembrance every now and again but you have to boldly speak back to him and let him know that you've already been forgiven for those things. Not only that, but also that you freely receive God's grace and mercy so get behind me satan. I encourage you to get a few scriptures that you can write on your mirror so you can speak the Word of God back to satan. Jesus Christ did this when He was tempted by satan, and it worked.

My hope is that if you're reading this book, you have some desire to break free not just from pornography addiction but also lust and perversion. In your process, there are going to be times where you fall short and mess up. That looks differently for each individual person, but we are all human beings who make mistakes. We wouldn't need Jesus if we had it all together. So, whenever you have a day where you fall short (sin), what you need to do is IMMEDIATELY go to God humbly, confess your sin, and ask Him to forgive you. Repent and let Him know that you are turning away from that sin. Also ask God to help you to change; confess that you are weak, and you need His strength to come upon you. 2 Corinthians 12:9 says, "But he said to me, "My grace is sufficient for you, for my power is made perfect in weakness." Therefore, I will boast all the more gladly about my weaknesses, so that Christ's power may rest on me." Boasting or confessing your weakness will be very crucial in your process. Honestly, I do this anytime I sin so that satan has no room to try and guilt me. We have to trust that our slate is wiped clean and God is willing to give us another chance to get it right. I always thank the Lord for second chances.

One thing that I'm learning is that on this journey having people around you who will support you even when you fall is important. Maybe you don't have people around you who could really help you in this way. This problem is easy, all you have to do is ask God to bring people in your life that can help you along the way. For example, when I was a Freshmen in college, I had a roommate who was a Sophomore. She would let me hang out with her and her friends, but I eventually felt like I was forcing myself to be someone I wasn't because I couldn't be myself around them. So, I prayed and asked God to bring me godly friends that I could hang around. I even asked God to help me to be more friendly to receive those friends. I was very introverted.

Being that way didn't help me make friends because I wouldn't let anyone in. God answered my prayer. About 2 months after praying that prayer I met one of my best friends for the rest of my college years. Prayer works.

In Revelations 12:11 it says, "And they have defeated him by the blood of the Lamb and by their testimony…" The him in this scripture is satan and one way we can easily defeat him is by confessing our sins one to another. I know that it can be hard to be transparent about things like struggling with pornography, masturbation, etc. but when we remain quiet about it that's when the devil really tries to torment us. Even if we no longer struggle with it, he will try his best to still torture us. There is a point in our journey where we should not only confess our sins to one another, but when we come to a point of overcoming sin in our lives. We should share our testimony so that others may be encouraged. A lot of the things we go through in life and even put ourselves through, God wants to use for His glory. In Romans 8:28 it says, "And we know that God works all things together for the good of those who love Him, who are called according to His purpose." Never be ashamed of your story because one day, just like I was able to use my story to write this book, you will be able to use your story to help someone else break free from lust, perversion, and a pornography addiction. Even if you never get to tell your story on a stage, as long as you're able to help at least one person, that's all that matters.

Being faithful with helping one means so much more than desiring a big platform to help many, especially when God hasn't called you to that. If God has called, you to a big platform then that's awesome also. Most importantly, just be sure to pour into others whether you have one or many. I never thought that I would want to help one person let alone a number of people through my story but here I am because God has led me here. I honestly would have preferred to be in the background and to stay quiet about my testimony.

Then one day, I felt led to open up about it and it encouraged so many others to want to share as well. I found out that when you are bold about your story, it helps others be bold. That's a special experience we get to have with others. Somehow, we all seem to get peace knowing that someone else has been through what you have been through. There is peace in godly unity. As a believer in Jesus Christ I am ready to stop being afraid to share my struggles with others and feeling the need to put on this mask acting like I am perfect. The truth is we aren't perfect, and we never will be. THAT IS OKAY because it's through our struggles God is able to get the glory in ways we can't even imagine. Don't discount your story. Don't discount your struggles. Don't discount your past because someone needs what you learned from it. That someone may even be me. I believe that we all have something to share to help our brother or our sister but what good is it if we keep it to ourselves?

One Step to a Porn Free Life

Reflections
Questions

1. Can you recall key moments where someone spoke into your life? What did they say? Did you believe them?

2. If someone said something to you or about you that was a lie, how would you react? What would you do to make sure you didn't believe the lie yourself?

3. If someone asked you who you are, what would you tell them?

Reflections

One Step to a Porn Free Life
Reflections

QUIANDRA JAMES

5
BAGGAGE CLAIM

Whenever you come off an airplane, there is usually baggage that you have to claim before you leave the airport. At baggage claim you usually wait to see your baggage on the conveyor belt, then once you spot it you go pick it up. So, I want to dig a little deeper with you and ask what baggage are you claiming?

I'll start with me. Four years into my journey of being free from my pornography addiction and even though I have not had a desire to watch porn since that day I made a promise to God, I found myself still dealing with the residue of years of watching porn. Certain words would trigger me into remembering names and scenes that I've watched in the past.

There was a lot of battling with my mind because pornography was my distraction from thinking about life. Once I and think about the lives of others. I had to digest what I really thought about myself, about how I viewed other people, and about the negative words I spoke about others. I had baggage. It annoyed me so much that all I could do was to QUICKLY ask God to renew my mind (please read Romans 12:2 and Ephesians 4:23). I recognized that even though I had baggage, I had to claim it and then quickly give it to God. I continued this for a while and it worked every single time because I made sure to speak out loud, "Lord I need Jesus to help me remain free, this is nothing I can do in my own strength." What I was saying was, "Lord I have baggage, but this is not mine to claim anymore so I take it, but I give it to you. Please replace this with something of yours." I know I wanted God to replace my baggage with His love, joy, peace, forgiveness, self-control, humility, compassion, freedom, gentleness, hope, faith, deliverance, healing, patience, kindness, long-suffering, understanding, wisdom, and discernment. I needed help.

God heard my cry and even helped me to know what my baggage was. I had to put a name on it. One day I ran across this website called Marriedandyoung.com. I followed their blog for a while and then I saw they were starting this program called The One University. I became a member of this program created by the founders of Married and Young

One Step to a Porn Free Life

Natasha and Jamal Miller. In their program they have 7 stages that you go through that helps you become the one for your future spouse. What I loved most about the program is that it is all centered around Christ. They made sure that before they even discussed becoming the one for another man or woman, we become focused on pursuing God as well as becoming whole. Send me an email if you would like their information. Long story short, in the midst of doing this program, I realized that there was some actual baggage I needed to claim that I didn't know was mine.

That baggage was called soul ties. Soul ties I had with the porn stars I watched. I legit didn't think this was a thing. I know I discussed this in an earlier chapter, but I want to go a little deeper here. I realized that the soul ties I had with porn stars were some of the causes for the thought patterns I described above. If you've watched porn stars for years like I have, there is literally a change that takes place in you through the people you are watching. These porn stars made me compare myself to them physically. I didn't see myself as beautiful and I began to believe that being beautiful meant that a man desired me sexually. I started to lust after women and my thought patterns were just spiraling downward. Porn stars became the company I kept and so their ways became my ways and their desires became my desires. When someone's soul is tied or attached to yours, they are able to influence you in a variety of ways. Even to the point where you would lose your marriage, leave your family, lose your job, fight someone, or move to another state over them. How many of us have had sex with someone that was not our spouse and then they did something to hurt us, but we kept going back to them? That is considered a soul tie because they were able to influence you even though what they did to you was wrong. I have stayed in relationships with people because of a soul tie even though I knew they weren't any good for me. That's influence, that's bad influence.

I want you to take some time and get in a quiet space without any distractions. I want you to get in a space where you are really comfortable. I want you to get your pen and your notebook. This is a time to be real and extremely honest with yourself. Think about this: In watching pornography, have you noticed any aspects of yourself where pornography has influenced you? What aspects have you seen watching pornography has influenced who you are today? Evaluate the person you are when you don't watch pornography compared to the person you are when you do. For those who quickly say that pornography has not influenced you, I want you to think about this. If pornography didn't control you, would you need to get free from it?

1 Corinthians 6:16-20 describes it perfectly, but let's break it down. It says, "Do you not know that he who unites himself with a prostitute is one with her in body? For it is

said, "The two will become one flesh." 17 But whoever is united with the Lord is one with him in spirit. 18 Flee from sexual immorality. All other sins a person commits are outside the body, but whoever sins sexually, sins against their own body. 19 Do you not know that your bodies are temples of the Holy Spirit, who is in you, whom you have received from God? You are not your own; 20 you were bought at a price. Therefore, honor God with your bodies." (NIV)

If you think about it, essentially when you're watching a pornographic movie you are watching 2 prostitutes have sex for some sort of material gain. With you watching them, you are joining in on what they are doing. Some people would love to say that this scripture is only talking about physically uniting yourself with a prostitute, but let's look at the word join. In the New International Version of the Bible, verse 16 says "Do you not know that he who unites himself with a prostitute is one with her in body? For it is said, 'The two will become one flesh.' Now in the King James Version of the Bible it uses the word join, instead of unites, which in Greek means to keep company, to stick, to glue, or to cement. When you're watching pornography, you're not only uniting your soul with those people but you're taking on all of the soul ties they already have. Can you imagine how many soul ties porn stars have? With you just watching it has given satan access to allow your soul to be bonded to theirs, and all of their soul ties. Have you ever had a friend come to you and they are upset because the person they are dating just hurt them? Being transparent, when my friends came to me with that type of situation, I was ready to go slash tires; that was the old me. Because I was bonded to them that meant our souls were tied together, and because our souls were tied together that meant that they had influence over me. Watching pornography bonds your soul to a porn star. Another form of bonding the soul with a porn star is the fantasizing or imagining. That is usually done when watching pornography or using it for sexual pleasure.

I am just going to tell on myself. I definitely imagined and fantasized about sex more than I have actually had sex. That is how much influence watching pornography had on me. So, when I stopped, I had to deal with the imaginations. Even though I have not watched any pornography throughout these four years, I still found myself remembering a pornographic scene; until I broke the soul ties, I had with those porn stars. That is influence. God's Word says, "Casting down imaginations, and every high thing that exalteth itself against the knowledge of God and bringing into captivity every thought to the obedience of Christ." (2 Corinthians 10:5 KJV) That means when your imagination is not lined up with the baggage, as I mentioned earlier, it is lined up with how satan wants you to live. The enemy wants you to think thoughts that are not like God and distract you from being more like Christ. I spoke this scripture, and still do, over and over until my imaginations obeyed God. I no longer wanted pornography or anything lustful to have my mind, but I wanted God to have it. Satan knows that if he can get your mind then the rest of our body parts will follow. But if we can submit our mind to Jesus Christ, the living Word, then we can make our other body parts follow. Submitting to Jesus Christ is simple. It is just how I described earlier, saying "God I have this baggage. I am claiming that I struggle with lust. I put a name on it. Now God will you please help me. I am weak in this area and I need you to make me strong."

The effects of a soul tie are a never-ending cycle when you're in it. Once you realize you have a soul tie you have to release yourself from those soul ties that was created in order to be free from them. It first starts with asking God for forgiveness and confessing it as sin, that you allowed others who weren't your husband/wife or God to be bonded to you in a soul tie. Repent with a remorseful heart for watching pornography because we don't realize that our sin actually hurts God just like us acting up as a kid hurts our parents. After you pray that prayer, then you should pray prayers that release you from those soul ties.

I suggest you take the time right now to write down names of porn stars you have watched (I watched so many that I also listed categories of porn I watched). The next thing I suggest you do is forgive those porn stars for the part they played in you sinning. Pray for those people. This can be whatever you feel God leads you to pray. I usually release them and speak blessings, favor, and prosperity over their lives. I suggest even praying that God would deliver them from working in the pornography industry and that God would open their eyes to see their line of work the way God sees it. Finally, ask God to cut any ungodly soul ties formed between yourself and porn stars as a result of you watching porn. I suggest you say their names while you are praying to be released from them. Finally, pray that in Jesus Christ name and then submit that to God with an AMEN.

This is a moment where it's just you and God, where you just release to Him all of that baggage you've been holding onto. Whether it was guilt, shame, living a double life, lying all the time to cover up your sin, being a cold person after you watch porn, being a mean person, or whatever it may be. Whatever it is, God wants to take all that which came to you as a result of you watching pornography. My testimony was not that I claimed my baggage in the beginning of my journey because I didn't really give God time to deal with me that deeply, I just went straight to working on doing my part. Which I believe was the right thing to do to some extent because I wanted to keep my word to God. However, I ended up later having to go through the process of God dealing with the baggage that came with my pornography addiction. Now that I know, I'm letting you guys into my learning experiences, so that you can learn from my mistakes. Please take this wisdom and take the time to do your part in claiming your baggage. Then give that baggage to Jesus Christ. Only He knows what to do with it. I promise He won't let you down. He has not let me down yet, and He never will.

Reflections
Questions

1. Identify areas in your life where you need to claim your baggage. If you aren't sure, please read Galatians 5:16-26 as a reference.

2. After answering questions from this chapter, what are some necessary steps you feel you need to take to properly move forward?

3. Do you believe that your baggage is not too much for God to handle? If so, why? If not, why not?

One Step to a Porn Free Life
Reflections

Reflections

One Step to a Porn Free Life

QUIANDRA JAMES

6
WHAT'S THAT SMELL?

Have you ever thought why you even have baggage? Of course, pornography can cause baggage but what else? Every chapter I want to go deeper until we get to the very root of your pornography addiction. Only then will you be able to uproot everything that has kept you in enslaved to pornography. I want you to picture this. Have you ever been around someone who have what you believe to be a bad odor, but it's early in the morning so you know that there's a chance it's not because they didn't take a bath? How about someone that breath smells bad but it's 9 o'clock in the morning? I am not trying to be funny; I am trying to get you to visualize my point. Stick with me. To that person, it's highly likely that they have no clue that they even have an odor or that their breath stinks, so it's almost as if everyone can smell it but them. That's how it is when you don't deal with the root cause of your addictions and bad habits. When I stopped watching pornography, I felt free, but I was a very judgmental person because I had insecurities that I never dealt with. You guys, I smelled bad and didn't know it. I was tooting my nose up at other people for not being perfect when I had insecurities myself.

Not only that, I was putting my own insecurities onto others. I wish someone would have told me how bad I smelled, but that's okay because God told me during my freedom journey. So, I am going to do you a favor and tell you something that nobody else may have the guts to say to your face. You smell, and it's not a good smell. I know I don't know you but, in a sense, I do know you because I have been you. Since you have not dealt with the root of your pornography addiction you either find yourself angry often, you get offended easily, you judge others, you struggle with forgiving other people, you have a hard time trusting people to help you, you find yourself overeating, and the list can go on. Because you have not dealt with the root of your pornography addiction, there is something lingering on you that is hindering you from being completely free and healed. This may be the hardest part of this journey because you have to really take your time to evaluate your life from childhood until now. The good news is that we are in this together, there is no rush, and you are free to go at your own pace. All of this I am teaching you is something that I learned in a matter of 5 years, and to be honest I am still learning things. So, we are just going to take this one step at a time.

When you're dealing with pornography, there is always a root issue that leads you to that place of becoming addicted to it. That means dealing with being rejected, being bullied for being different, daddy and mommy issues, unforgiveness, bitterness from maybe someone who molested or raped you as a child, maybe rebellion because you never dealt with the pain of your parents divorcing and feeling it was your fault, etc. YOU HAVE TO HEAL. One thing I really struggled with after being free was believing, even though I was forgiven by God and that God still loved me. I really had it in my mind that any little mess up I made; God was ready to whoop me. That came from that perfectionist mentality that as long as I had control and was this perfect person, God loved me. If I worked hard enough Jesus would always love me and would never be disappointed in me. I even believed this after being freed from my addiction. Any little or big sin I did caused me to hide from God because I thought He was ready to punish me due to my lack of perfection. So, then I found myself not reading the Bible, not wanting to go to church, and basically not wanting to have anything to do with God because I thought He didn't want anything to do with me. It was almost as if I thought God would reject me, so I tried to reject Him first. That was a lie straight from satan. Not only was it a lie but it was one of the things that drove me to watch pornography. I recognized that this was an insecurity of not being good enough, that was the root. A root that wasn't God's fault. It was something that started from my parents. Anytime I made a mistake, as a child, my dads (I have 2) were so quick to come at me in a very performing way. A performance father figure is a father where, their premise is "I award you when you are perfect, and I punish as well as reject you when you aren't." Now I know my dads were trying to correct me because they loved me, but it was how they did it that caused me to not be able to receive what they were really doing. I felt like I could never do anything right for my dads. That bled into my relationship with God where I felt like I could never do anything right for Him. If you have ever felt this way, I want you to know God loves you, regardless of if you choose Him or not. Jesus Christ died on the cross because He loved us ALL, even the ones who are unbelievers in Him right now. He died for us even before we decided to believe in Him. There is nothing you can do that can take away the love God has for you. You can't work for Christ's love! It's a free gift that God has just waiting for you to receive. You won't really know that until you go through a process of coming into agreement with being a son of God. Now what is being a son of God? I'm glad you asked. As a believer in Christ Jesus, being a son of God is simple. God's Word says in Galatians 4:4-7, "But when the right time came, God sent his Son, born of a woman [Mary], subject to the law [living by the law of the earth]. 5 God sent him to buy freedom for us who were slaves to the law, so that he could adopt us as his very own children. 6 And because we are his children, God has sent the Spirit of his Son into our hearts, prompting us to call out, "Abba, Father." 7 Now you are no longer a slave but God's own child. And since you are his child, God has made you his heir." There is a lot of elements to this scripture but what I want you to visualize is that God loved you so much that He sent His Son Jesus Christ to come down from the most beautiful and perfect place, heaven, to be on earth so that we can know who God is as our Father. Just take the time to think about that. Think about your child, if you have one. If you were God, wouldn't you do the same thing to save your child and let your child know that you loved them so much you would leave the comfort of heaven so that they would know you? I can't lie, I don't know if I would but then again, that's why I'm not God. But God, the Creator of heaven and earth thought of us that much. He wanted to do whatever it took for us to know that He loved us and that we were His children. So, the first requirement to be a son of God is making Jesus Christ your Lord and Savior. The second step is telling God that you receive Him as your Father and that you are now His son. The third step is asking God to show you how to receive Him as a Father, how to receive His love, and how to be a son. I would give you examples, but I think this is a personal journey God wants to have between you and Him. A unique experience and adventure with your Father. I will however have some recommended books that you can email me about.

Another thing that I had to deal with along this journey was rejection. I realized that there is a root issue to rejection. I want you to take some time and get your pen and paper. Now I want you to think about the times that you have felt rejected, and I want you to write them down. Think about why you felt rejected in those moments and write those down. Okay, so let's discuss this. I am going to talk about my own life. On this journey I have realized that the reason I have felt rejected by so many people in my past was because I was DIFFERENT. Can you relate to that?

The root issue was identity. I could remember making remarks that I thought were hilarious, but no one would laugh, it was because I was different. I could also remember the times I tried to hang with the cool crowd, but I never felt comfortable with them nor did they receive me. There were times I wanted to date guys, but no one wanted to date me. It was all because I was different. Even though I was different, I didn't want to be. I wanted to be like everybody else. God showed me that all those times, what He was trying to get me to see was that He allowed those people to reject me because I was different. That meant I couldn't just hang out with anybody, I couldn't just date anybody, and I couldn't just say anything I wanted to say. That just wasn't me even though I wanted it to be me so badly, so others could accept me. Because I was different and couldn't accept that I was different, I ran to pornography. Pornography always made me "feel" wanted and it always made me "feel" like I belonged. Until God showed me one day that yes, I am different, but it is not a bad thing to be different. In fact, there is nobody else in the world like me and that is not something to be ashamed of. I needed to be excited about who God created me to be because He took special time creating me just the way that I am. I want you to see the same thing. Even though you are different, you are just who God created you to be. He took special time out to carefully make you. He cares that much about you. If you are in a comfortable space, I want you to take the time to say a short prayer to Jesus.

"Lord, thank you for making me different. Thank you for taking our time to make me and making me like you. I ask Lord that you help me to love myself the way you made me. I ask God that you help me to find joy in being who you created me to be. Even when there are times when I don't know who I am God I ask that you show me who you say I am. I want to believe what you say over how I feel, or the negative things others have said about me.

Lord, I ask that you help me. In Jesus Christ name I pray amen."

This is not an exhaustive list of root issues, but these are root issues I feel are really important to address. The last root issue I want to discuss is trauma. That trauma could be being molested or raped by someone, getting into a car accident, betrayal, being in a war, getting shot, seeing someone get killed, getting a disease, being abused in any way, or anything that drastically alters the course of your life. Trauma is a root issue that many people shy away from addressing because it causes you to have to go back and relive those moments. I honestly think this is a root issue that you should address with a mentor and/or Christian Counselor.

You need someone to walk this out with who is loving and patient with your process. I encourage you to not be afraid to open up about this because in your journey of freedom, you will be surprised how opening up helps you to be a better wife/husband, parent, friend, and all around just a better you for yourself. I see trauma as a root issue in pornography addiction due to so many people using pornography as a distraction from the thoughts of the trauma and a way to escape; using pornography to numb the pain and the hurt that the trauma might have caused. Some people even get into the pornography industry because of the trauma that they have never dealt with, and sex was a way to numb the pain. If this is you, I want you to know that you are not alone. Whoever may be reading this, and you are thinking that it's not easy to deal with the trauma, I also want you to know that you are right...it's not easy.

It won't be but I can promise you that as you continue to discuss the trauma and get an outside perspective on how to heal from it, it gets easier. The process will be worth it. Maybe one day you will get to help others walk through their process just like someone helped you. That brings purpose to your pain. God's word says in Genesis 50:20, "Don't you see, you planned evil against me, but God used those same plans for my good, as you see all around you right now—life for many people." Though people do things that cause us pain, those very same things can be used to help others. Even though I would have preferred that my family members did not introduce me to pornography, God has used it to help so many people. One last thing I want you to take time to do when pondering on this root issue, is to forgive God because you might have felt like He was not there to protect you from this trauma.

Even though God does not need our forgiveness, there are times where we have to free our conscious and forgive God for something that we are holding against Him in our hearts. God loves us and will never do anything to hurt us. But we experience hurt because all human beings have a free will, and unfortunately, we all have used that free will to hurt someone. It's not God's fault we were involved in a trauma. No matter how much our mind wants us to believe that it is God's fault, it is not.

I can be honest and say when I have experienced trauma, I asked God: Where were you Lord? Why didn't you protect me? He reassured me that He was always there, and He did protect me because He kept me from dying. That trauma was meant to kill you, but God shielded you and is wanting to use that trauma for good. Now I want you to stop and breath.

This is a tough topic, but I want you to take a piece of paper and a pen. I want you to just write what you are feeling in this moment. Write out whatever is on your mind. If you feel like crying, cry. If you feel like screaming, scream. Whatever it is, don't hold it in. You have held all of this in long enough. You are not the victim anymore. You may even need to say that to yourself until you believe it. It is time to allow yourself to address how you feel and get it out. Then ask God what you do from here. I would give you some suggestions but again I think this should be a personal time with just you and God. Even if you feel you don't hear anything, just rest in His presence. He is there with you, right now. Let Him comfort you. Even if you shed a tear or two and don't say a word, guess what? God can hear you. He knows what you are trying to give to Him. No more holding it in. It's time to release it and make room for the brand-new things God is wanting to give you.

Reflections
Questions

1. Considering the root of your pornography addiction. What stands out as the more surprising element?

2. This is a time of releasing for you. Who and what are some things that you are committing to letting go off today?

3. What are the new things you are looking forward to receiving from God?

One Step to a Porn Free Life
Reflections

Reflections

One Step to a Porn Free Life

QUIANDRA JAMES

7
CONCLUSION

You made it to the end alive! Now you have some work to do but the beautiful thing is God is with you. At this point you should have thought of some people who could support you along this journey, and you can find comfort that there are others like you reading this book also wanting to break free. You are not alone and anytime that lie comes across your mind, just remind yourself of the things I spoke of above. I want to end on this note.

I want you to right now close your eyes and begin to imagine Jesus Christ being whipped, being spit on, being chained, being nailed on the cross, and being pierced in his side for you.

I really want you to meditate on this and how you picture this looked to you, a totally innocent man who said you were worth it to go through all of that for. Do you feel the love of God right now? Do you feel the unworthiness of His Son choosing to live a perfect life and die for you and me? The truth is we are unworthy but that didn't stop Him from saying we are worth it. So anytime you find yourself at a low point, where you are one click away from watching porn after you haven't looked at it in 7 months, you're wanting to masturbate, you're wanting to have sex outside of marriage because porn has tempted you to try something "different", or whatever your situation may be, I want you to take some time to imagine Jesus Christ's process of dying on the cross for your sins.

I will never scare you into believing you need to do what God commands us to do because it doesn't work. What I will do though, is make you consider how much God loves you which will then make you ponder if you really love God. Can you pursue living a holy life like His Son Jesus. Again, you have reinforcements such as your friends. If you feel an urge, call your accountability partner and ask if you guys can go out somewhere or go shoot some hoops, whatever works for you. We also have the Holy Spirit. If you aren't sure you have the Holy Spirit, I would suggest researching in the Bible what the Holy Spirit is and His functions.

Also, I suggest going to your local church and telling the Pastor you want to be filled with the Holy Spirit. Or you could just decide to spend time with God alone and just ask Him to fill you with His Holy Spirit. This is a huge act of faith, so all you have to do is believe that God will grant whatever you ask Him for. God is doing amazing things in your life and I hope you are excited to be forever changed, not just for yourself but for your future generations. You are worth it, your future/present seeds are worth it, and Jesus Christ is worth it.

Reflections
Questions

1. There will be challenges throughout this journey. It doesn't end when you finish reading this book. What scriptures will you use to combat those challenges and that will keep you encouraged?

2. What have you learned about yourself?

3. How will you encourage others in their journey of becoming free from pornography addiction or any life challenges?

One Step to a Porn Free Life
Reflections

Reflections

One Step to a Porn Free Life

MEET THE AUTHOR

Quiandra E. James is a wife, daughter, a sister, a niece, a granddaughter, and a child of God. These qualities are her highest achievements. As a Social Worker, she has everyday interactions with families and individuals to offer a wise action plan that will support and improve their quality of life.

Quiandra is creative and unique in the way she offers helpful advice to many families as they cope with social challenges. Her heart is to lead God's people to Him one creative project at a time. This platform allows her to share the love of Jesus Christ with groups and communities in an effort to help people overcome some of life's most difficult problems and enhance their overall well-being.

Visit her website for more information www.callquiandra.com or email her at quiandraegrant@gmail.com.

QUIANDRA JAMES

One Step to a Porn Free Life

Contact Author

Want to schedule a book signing or speaking event, or submit confidential questions to the author?

Complete the contact form at
www.callquiandra.com

Social Media:
Instagram @quiandrajames
Facebook @ Quiandra James

You Want to Write a Book?

Contact our publisher at
www.drnesintl.com

QUIANDRA JAMES

Contact Author

Want to schedule a book signing or speaking event, or submit confidential questions to the author?

Complete the contact form at www.xxx.xx

www.ingramcontent.com/pod-product-compliance
Lightning Source LLC
Chambersburg PA
CBHW071155090426
42736CB00012B/2340